Ikenaga 2 Jos Leys

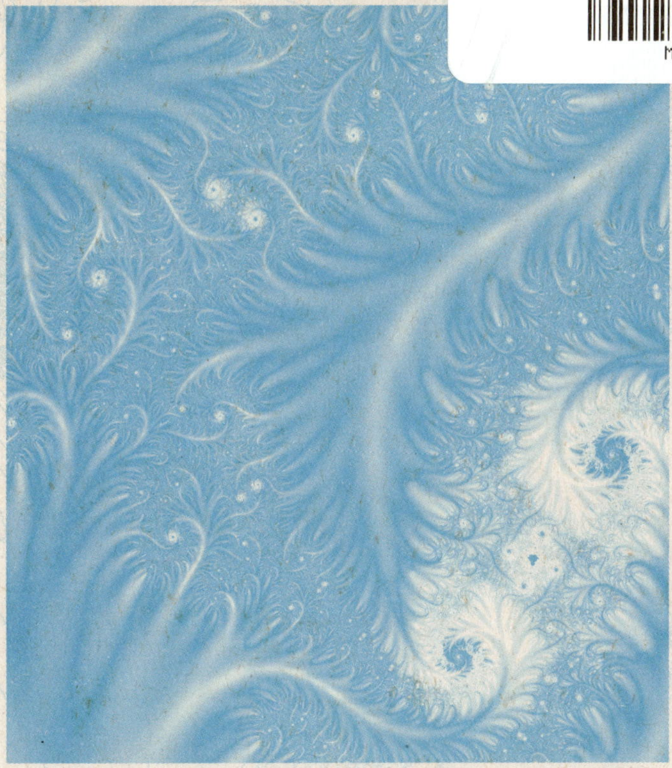

"A relatively simple formula can generate immensely complex images." – Jos Leys

Student Activity Book

Perimeter, Angles, and Area

UNIT 4

Investigations

IN NUMBER, DATA, AND SPACE®

Editorial offices: Glenview, Illinois • Parsippany, New Jersey • New York, New York
Sales offices: Boston, Massachusetts • Duluth, Georgia
Glenview, Illinois • Coppell, Texas • Sacramento, California • Mesa, Arizona

The Investigations curriculum was developed by TERC, Cambridge, MA.

This material is based on work supported by the National Science Foundation ("NSF") under Grant No.ESI-0095450. Any opinions, findings, and conclusions or recommendations expressed in this material are those of the author(s) and do not necessarily reflect the views of the National Science Foundation.

ISBN: 0-328-24047-8

ISBN: 978-0-328-24047-0

17-V011-16 15 14

Perimeter, Angles, and Area

Investigation 1

Investigation 2

Investigation 3

Name Date

Finding Lengths

Use a ruler, yardstick, and meterstick to find objects that are about the same length as these measurement units. Record the objects that you find for each unit.

Centimeter	Inch
Example: The tip of my pencil	

Foot	Yard/Meter

What's the Number?

Answer the following questions.

NOTE Students work on place value in 3-digit numbers.

SMH **7–8, 9, 36**

1. What number is 50 more than 824? ________
2. What number is 40 less than 567? ________
3. What number is 80 more than 365? ________
4. What number is 30 less than 215? ________
5. What number is 200 more than 439? ________
6. What number has 5 hundreds, 3 tens, and 2 ones? ________
7. What number has 31 tens and no ones? ________
8. What number has 6 hundreds and 8 ones? ________
9. What number has 4 hundreds and 13 tens? ________
10. What number has 16 tens and 15 ones? ________

Choosing Measurement Tools and Units (page 1 of 2)

NOTE Students decide which measuring tools are most appropriate for each situation. Students will continue to measure lengths in class for the next few days.

SMH 105, 106, 107

What measurement tool (ruler, yardstick, or meterstick) would you use for each situation? What unit of measure (centimeter, inch, foot, yard, or meter) would you use?

Explain why you chose that tool and that unit of measure.

1. I need to know the length of a fence that will go around the basketball court.

Tool: ________________ Unit of Measure: ________________

I chose these because . . .

2. I need to know how long the strap is on my book bag.

Tool: ________________ Unit of Measure: ________________

I chose these because . . .

Choosing Measurement Tools and Units (page 2 of 2)

3. I need to know the width of my foot at its widest point.

Tool: ________________ Unit of Measure: ________________

I chose these because . . .

4. I want to buy material for a bedspread. I need to know how long and how wide my bed is.

Tool: ________________ Unit of Measure: ________________

I chose these because . . .

Finding and Measuring Perimeters (page 1 of 2)

Choose 5 objects in the classroom that have perimeters you can measure, such as a bulletin board, the top of a table, or the side of the teacher's desk. Measure their perimeters and record your work below.

Object	Drawing of What I Am Measuring	Perimeter
Example: Top of my desk	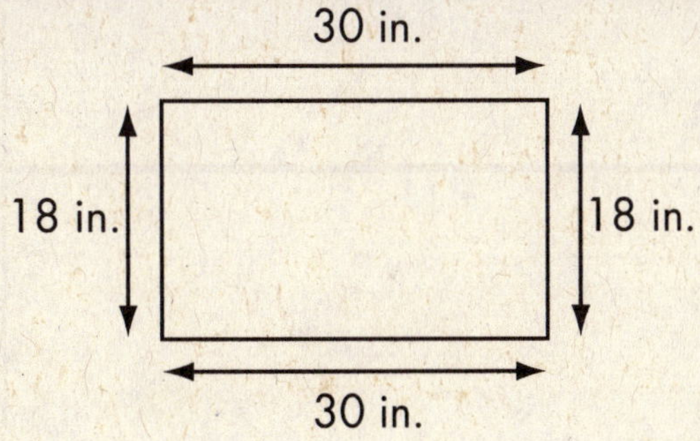	96 inches
1.		
2.		

Finding and Measuring Perimeters (page 2 of 2)

Object	Drawing of What I Am Measuring	Perimeter
3.		
4.		
5.		

Adding 10s and 100s

Solve the following sets of related problems. How would you use one problem to solve the next one?

NOTE Students practice solving addition problems in related sets.

SMH 20–24, 36

1. 168 + 30 = ________ 168 + 40 = ________ 168 + 50 = ________	**2.** 249 + 100 = ________ 249 + 200 = ________ 249 + 300 = ________
3. 67 + 40 = ________ 67 + 140 = ________ 67 + 240 = ________	**4.** 282 + 10 = ________ 282 + 20 = ________ 282 + 30 = ________
5. 206 + 30 = ________ 236 + 30 = ________ 266 + 30 = ________	**6.** 234 + 150 = ________ 234 + 160 = ________ 234 + 170 = ________

Name Date

Perimeters at Home

Measure the perimeters of at least two objects at home. Record your work below.

NOTE Students practice measuring the perimeter of objects, such as the top edge of the kitchen table or the front of the refrigerator door.

SMH 110–111, 112–113

Object	Drawing of What I Am Measuring	Perimeter

Perimeter Problems (page 1 of 2)

1. Your teacher wants to put a tape around the edge of the largest table in the classroom. How much tape will she need? Explain how you got the answer.

2. The perimeter of Pilar's yard is 100 feet. Draw a picture of what her yard might look like, and label each side.

Name Date

Perimeter Problems (page 2 of 2)

3. Draw three different rectangles below that each have a perimeter of 20 centimeters.

Name Date

Making Shapes

Draw a sketch of each given shape.
Label the length of each side.

NOTE Students draw and label shapes with given perimeters.

SMH 112

1. Square with a perimeter of 80 units	**2.** Rectangle with a perimeter of 120 units
3. Square with a perimeter of 160 units	**4.** Rectangle with a perimeter of 180 units

Ongoing Review

5. What is the perimeter of a square with 6-inch sides?

A. 12 **B.** 18 **C.** 24 **D.** 36

Name Date

Ordering Shapes by Perimeter (page 1 of 2)

1. Look at the shapes below. Put them in order from the shortest to the longest perimeter **without** measuring.

__________ __________ __________ __________

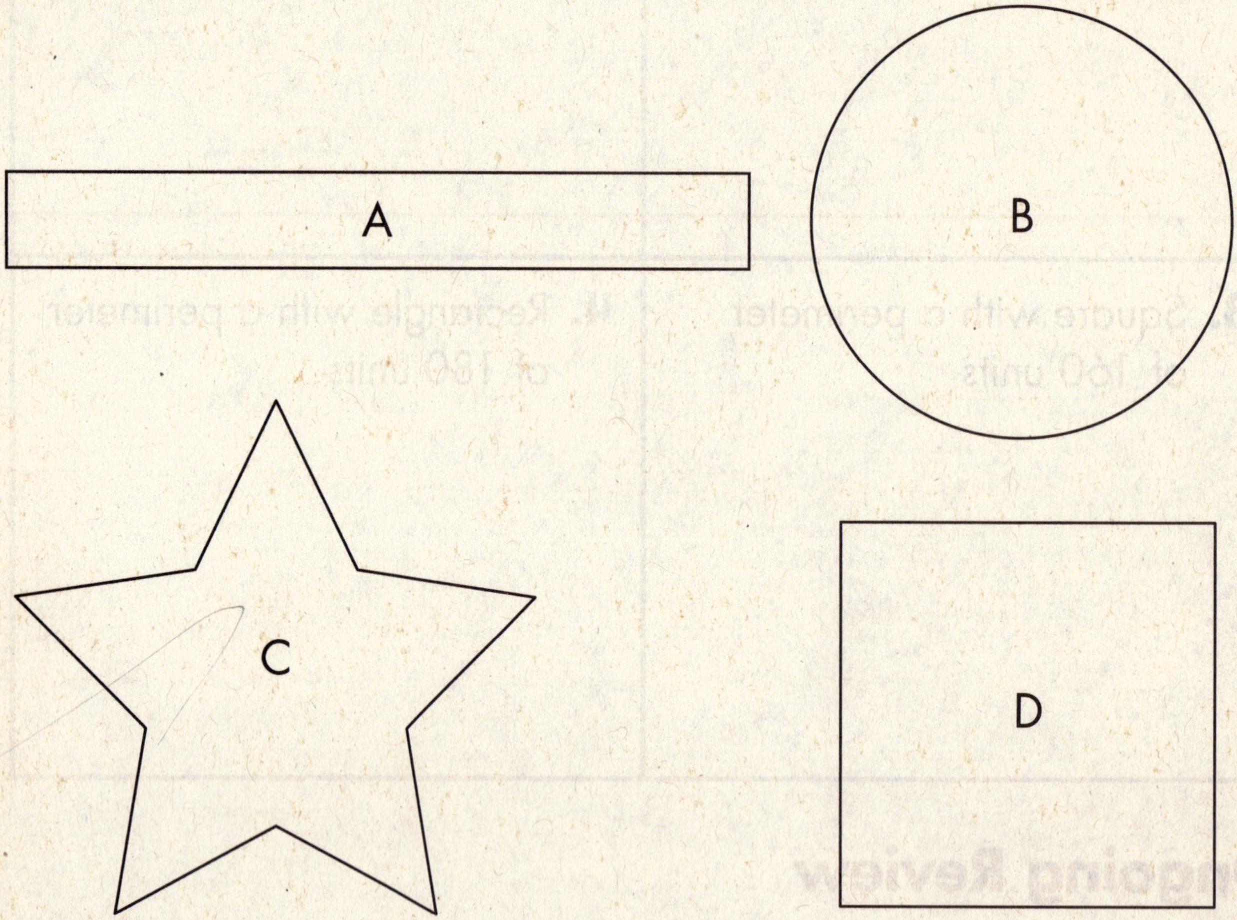

Name Date

Ordering Shapes by Perimeter (page 2 of 2)

2. Now choose a measurement tool and measure the perimeter of each shape. Put them in order from shortest to longest. Write the perimeter of each shape.

Measurement tool you chose: ______________________

________ ________ ________ ________

3. Compare the lists you made before and after you measured. Did anything surprise you about the perimeters of these shapes? Explain what you found out.

Name Date

Crossing Over 100

Solve the following sets of related problems. How would you use one problem to solve the next one?

NOTE Students practice solving subtraction problems in related sets.

SMH 32–35

1. 100 − 54 = ______ 110 − 54 = ______ 120 − 54 = ______	**2.** 100 − 86 = ______ 112 − 86 = ______ 132 − 86 = ______
3. 100 − 92 = ______ 121 − 92 = ______ 141 − 92 = ______	**4.** 100 − 37 = ______ 110 − 37 = ______ 120 − 37 = ______
5. 100 − 49 = ______ 120 − 49 = ______ 124 − 49 = ______	**6.** 100 − 83 = ______ 130 − 83 = ______ 138 − 83 = ______

Frog Jumps (page 1 of 2)

NOTE Students practice adding and subtracting centimeters.

SMH **25, 106**

1. Frogs A, B, C, and D had a jumping relay race. How many centimeters did they jump altogether?

2. Did they jump more or less than one meter? Explain how you know.

Frog Jumps (page 2 of 2)

3. Frogs E, F, G, and H are bullfrogs. How many centimeters did they jump altogether?

4. How much farther did they jump than Frogs A, B, C, and D?

Building Shapes

NOTE Students combine shapes and find the perimeter of the new shape.

SMH 110–111

Aaron combined two of these shapes to make a new shape.

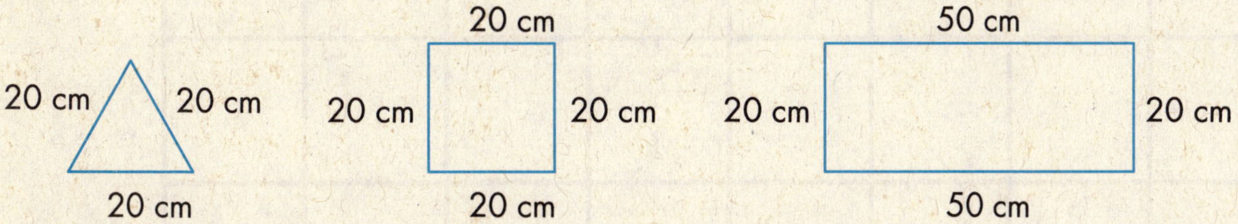

Here is the new shape Aaron made.

1. What is the perimeter of Aaron's new shape? ________

2. Combine the rectangle and the square.
Draw the new shape. Find the perimeter. ________

3. Combine the square and the triangle.
Draw the new shape. Find the perimeter. ________

8 × 10 Rectangle

The Perfect Cover-Up (page 1 of 2)

1. Choose one of the tetromino shapes. Draw the shape in the first column of the chart on the next page. Use 10–15 of that shape to cover as many squares as you can on the 8×10 rectangle on page 18.

2. Do you think this shape will completely cover the whole rectangle? How do you know? Answer this question in the second column of the chart.

3. If you are not sure whether it will cover the entire rectangle, you can do one of the following:
   a. Build more of the same tetromino shape and continue to cover the rectangle.
   b. On the rectangle, color the tetromino shapes you have already covered. Color all 4 squares in one tetromino shape the same color, but make each tetromino a different color. Then, try to cover the rest of the rectangle by moving the tetromino shapes or by coloring where additional tetrominoes will fit.

4. Answer the questions in the other columns of the chart.

5. Repeat these steps with the other tetromino shapes.

Name Date

The Perfect Cover-Up (page 2 of 2)

Tetromino Shape	Will it be a "perfect cover-up"? Yes or No	Why or why not?	How many cover the rectangle?

6. Which tetromino shapes were not a "perfect cover-up"? Explain why you think each one did not cover the 8 by 10 rectangle.

How Many More?

Solve the following problems and show your solutions on the number lines provided.

NOTE Students find the missing number to make an addition equation correct.

SMH 27

1. 116 + ________ = 250

2. 94 + ________ = 260

3. 143 + ________ = 300

4. 167 + ________ = 325

Addition Starter Problems

NOTE Students practice flexibility with solving addition problems.

SMH 20–24

Solve each problem two ways, using the first steps listed below. Show your work clearly.

1. 138 + 174 = ________

Start by solving 138 + 4.	Start by solving 130 + 170.

2. 259 + 163 = ________

Start by solving 200 + 100.	Start by solving 60 + 60.

Puzzle Pieces

Which pieces fit in the holes? Draw a line from each hole in the puzzle to the piece that will fit exactly. The pieces are painted on one side only. You can turn pieces, but do not flip them! Carefully cut out the pieces. Glue in place the ones that fit.

NOTE Students have been using flips, turns, and slides to compare shapes. On this page they find which puzzle pieces fit the puzzle.

SMH 117

Name Date

Tetromino Puzzle (page 1 of 2)

Name Date

Tetromino Puzzle (page 2 of 2)

Name Date

The Perfect Fit

> **NOTE** Students use puzzle pieces to practice geometry and spatial relationships.
>
> SMH 117

1. Draw a line from each hole in the puzzle to the piece that will fit there exactly. You can turn pieces, but do **not** flip them!

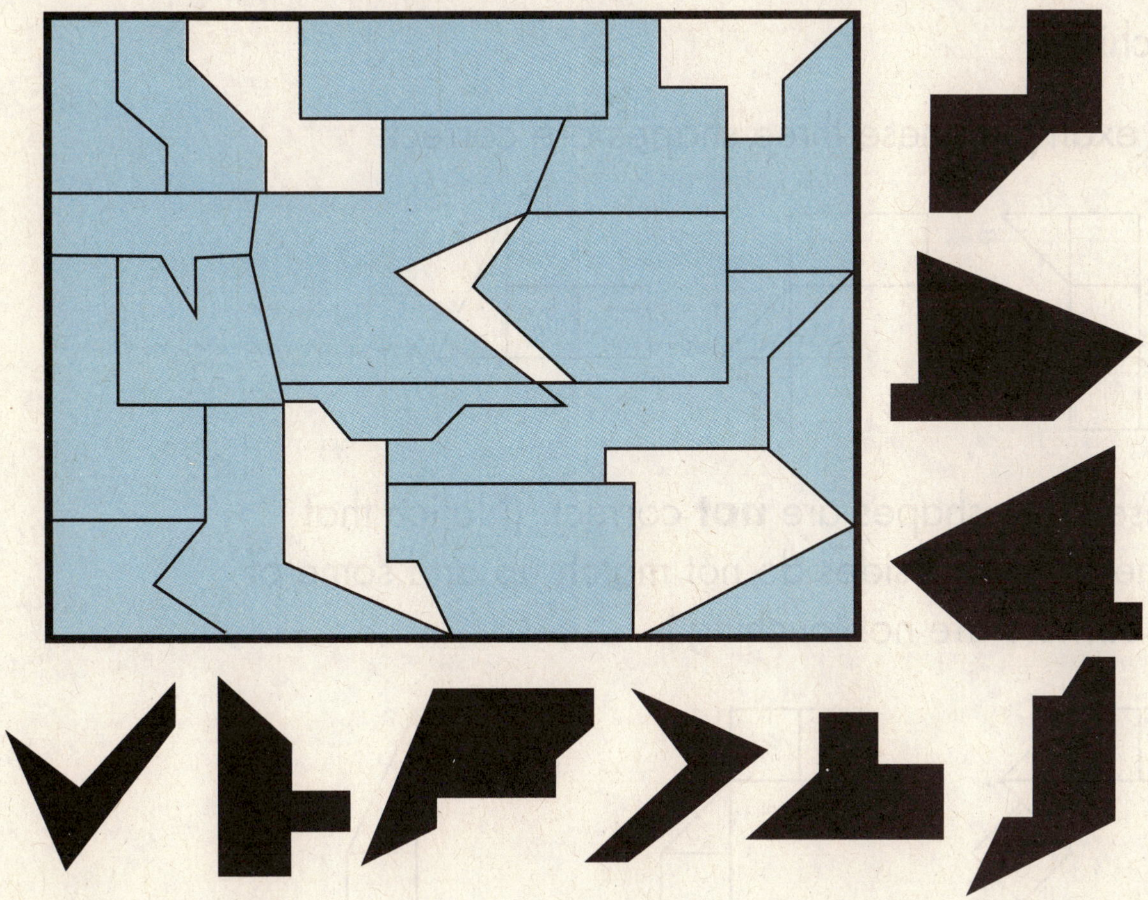

Ongoing Review

2. How was this tetromino moved?

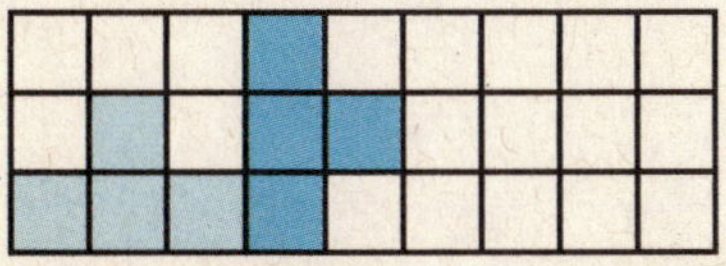

A. SLIDE **B.** TURN **C.** FLIP

Shape Poster

With your partner, use the Square and Triangle Cutouts (M17) to make new shapes with exactly 4 square units. Remember that each new shape must be like tetrominoes and have full sides touching.

For example, these three shapes are correct.

These three shapes are **not** correct. (Notice that some of the full sides do not match up and some of the corners are not touching.)

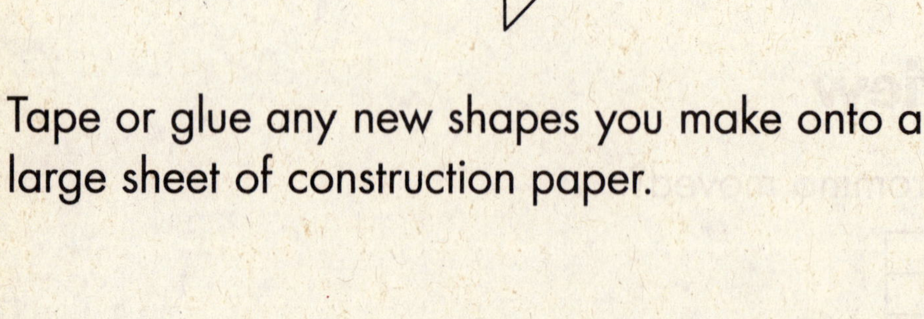

Tape or glue any new shapes you make onto a large sheet of construction paper.

Name Date

What's the Area? (page 1 of 2)

The drawings below show different sections of Mr. Tyler's room. Part of the tiled floor has been covered with a rug. Determine how many tiles are in the entire rectangle and explain how you found your answer.

1.

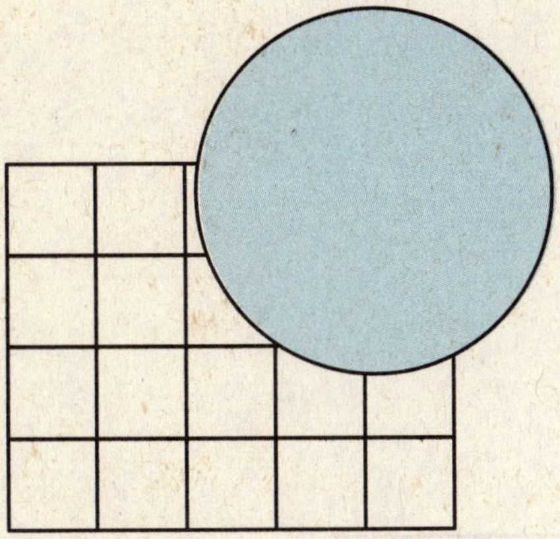

Area ________

2.

Area ________

What's the Area? (page 2 of 2)

3. 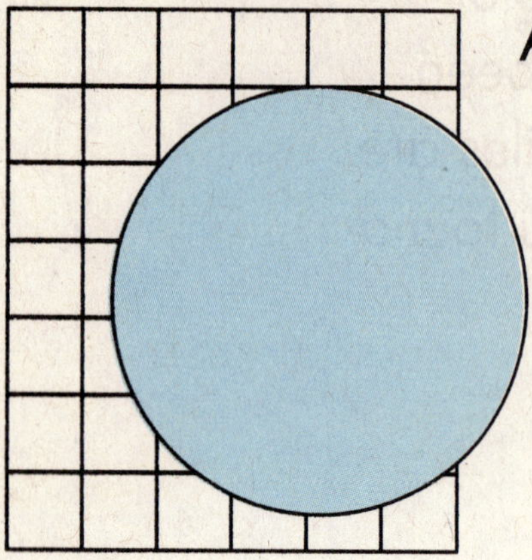

Area ________

4. 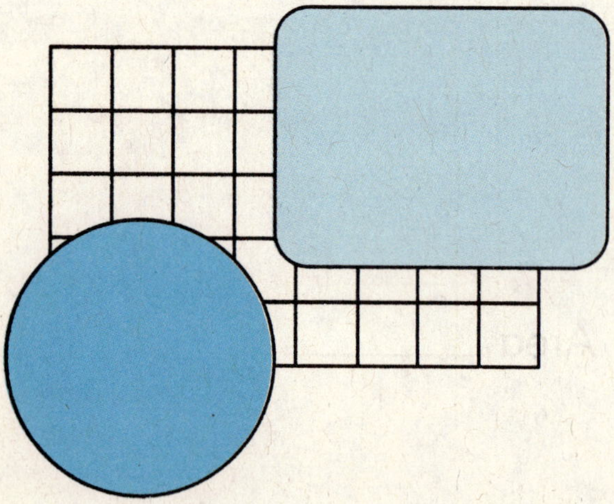

Area ________

Class Collections

NOTE Students find the difference between 3-digit numbers. Ask your child to explain how he or she solves each problem.

SMH 29–30, 32–35, 106

For each problem, write an equation, solve the problem, and show your solution. You may use a number line or your 1,000 chart to help you solve these problems.

1. The students in Ms. Ahmed's class are collecting bottle caps. Their goal is to collect 500. They have 317 so far. How many more do they need to reach their goal?

2. The students in Ms. Kennedy's class are collecting pennies. Their goal is to collect $7.00. So far they have 426 pennies. How many more do they need to reach their goal?

Ongoing Review

3. The perimeter of a rectangle is 39 centimeters. The perimeter of a circle is 39 inches. Which statement about the two shapes is correct?

   A. The rectangle has a larger perimeter.

   B. The circle has a larger perimeter.

   C. The rectangle and the circle have the same perimeter.

Make Some Frog Jumps

Answer the questions below, and explain how you solved the problem.

NOTE Students practice solving addition problems by finding 3 or 4 addends that equal the given sum.

SMH 25

1. Three frogs jumped a total of 115 centimeters. How far could each frog have jumped?

Frog 1______ Frog 2______ Frog 3______

How did you solve it?

2. Four frogs jumped a total of 185 centimeters. How far could each frog have jumped?

Frog 1_____ Frog 2_____ Frog 3_____ Frog 4_____

How did you solve it?

Name Date

How Big Is Your Foot?

Find the perimeter and area of your foot.
Then answer the following questions.

1. What is the perimeter of your foot?

Describe how you measured the perimeter.

2. What is the area of your foot?

Explain how you found your answer.

Seven-Unit Shapes

Use the Square and Triangle Cutouts (M17) to make three new shapes with an area of seven square units. Remember that each new shape must, like tetrominoes, have full sides touching.

NOTE Students build shapes with an area of 7 square units.

SMH 115

Tape or glue the new shapes you make on a large piece of paper. You may also draw the new shapes.

1. Use only squares in your first shape.

2. Use only triangles in your second shape.

3. Use both squares and triangles in your third shape.

Ongoing Review

4. What is the area of the following shape?

A. 2 square units

B. 3 square units

C. $3\frac{1}{2}$ square units

D. 4 square units

How Many 10s?

NOTE Students find groups of 10s in 3-digit numbers.

SMH 9

Solve each problem below. You may use your 1,000 chart to help you. Explain how you figured out each problem.

1. Mr. Jackson went to Sticker Station and bought strips of 10 stickers to give to his students. He bought 270 stickers. How many strips of 10 did he buy?

2. Ms. Donaldson's class has collected 375 stamps from old letters. They are displaying the stamps in rows of 10. How many rows can they make? How many stamps will be left over?

3. Ms. Vega's class is collecting bottle caps. They are displaying them in stacks of 10. So far they have 41 stacks of bottle caps and 3 single bottle caps. How many bottle caps do they have?

4. Philip and his sister are collecting pennies at home. They have 256 pennies so far. If they trade the pennies for dimes, how many dimes will they have? How many pennies will be left over?

Name Date

More Perimeter Problems

NOTE Students practice making rectangles and squares that have given perimeters.

SMH 112–113

1. Draw at least two different rectangles, each with a perimeter of 160 units. Label the length of each side.

2. My perimeter is 200. The length of one of my sides is 75. Draw the rest of my sides to make me a whole rectangle. Label the length of each side.

Name Date

Building Triangles (page 1 of 2)

Follow the directions below to make triangles with your straw building kit. Draw a picture of each triangle you make, and label the lengths of the straws you used for each side.

1. Make a triangle with all sides the same length.

2. Make a triangle from a 3-inch, a 4-inch, and a 5-inch straw.

Name Date

Building Triangles (page 2 of 2)

3. Make a triangle with two sides the same length and one side a different length.

4. Can you find three straws that will not make a triangle? Draw them and label their lengths. Why do you think they will not make a triangle?

Collecting Stickers and Pennies

NOTE Students practice solving addition problems that involve 2- and 3-digit numbers. Ask your child to explain how he or she solves each problem.

SMH 20–24

For each problem, write an equation, solve the problem, and show your solution.

1. Jung collects animal stickers. She has 158 stickers in her collection. On her birthday, her mother gave her 64 more stickers to add to her collection. How many animal stickers does Jung have now?

2. Oscar collects sports stickers. In his sticker box, he has 213 baseball stickers and 189 tennis stickers. How many of these sports stickers does Oscar have altogether?

3. Last month Kim collected 130 pennies. This month she collected 82 pennies. How much money does Kim have now?

4. Gil had 298 pennies in his collection. His younger sister had 112 pennies in her collection. They combined their collections to buy a present for their parents. How much money did they have altogether?

Tricky Triangles

Which Are Triangles? (page 1 of 2)

1. Which of the Tricky Triangles on page 40 are actually triangles? Without showing your partner, list the letter of each shape in the box below where you think it belongs.

These shapes are triangles:	These shapes are **not** triangles:

2. Now compare your list with your partner's. Discuss any shapes on which you disagree.

3. After you have discussed the Tricky Triangles with your partner, write why you think certain shapes are triangles and others are not triangles.

Which Are Triangles? (page 2 of 2)

4. Draw some shapes that are triangles and some that are **not** triangles. Then trade this sheet with your partner. Put the letter *T* in each shape your partner drew that is a triangle, and put the letters *NT* in each shape your partner drew that is **not** a triangle.

Make It a Triangle

Look at each shape below. Explain why these shapes are **not** triangles.

NOTE Students use their knowledge of properties of a triangle to explain why a shape is not a triangle.

SMH 118, 120

Shape	This shape is not a triangle because . . .
Example: 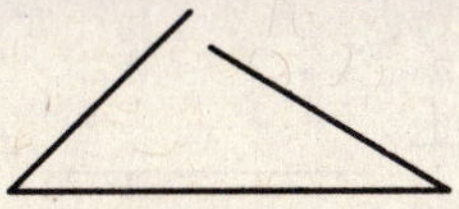	the sides are not closed.
1. 	
2. 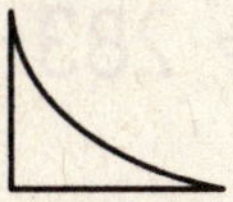	
3. 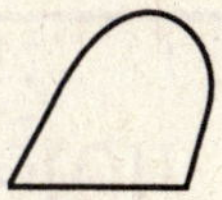	
4. 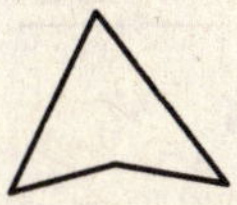	

Ongoing Review

5. Circle the correct statement about triangles.

A. Triangles have 4 sides.

B. Triangles must have a 90-degree angle.

C. Triangles have 3 vertices.

D. Triangles must have 3 equal sides.

Name Date

Related Problems

Solve the following sets of related problems. How would you use one problem to solve the next one?

NOTE Students practice solving addition and subtraction problems in related sets.

1. 250 − 100 = ______

250 − 90 = ______

250 − 95 = ______

250 − 105 = ______

2. 280 + ______ = 283

270 + ______ = 283

250 + ______ = 283

220 + ______ = 283

3. 53 + 47 = ______

153 + 147 = ______

253 + 147 = ______

253 + 247 = ______

4.

400	401	401
− 25	− 25	− 26

Name Date

Building Quadrilaterals (page 1 of 2)

Follow the directions below to make quadrilaterals with your straw building kit.

1. Make a square and a rectangle. Draw them here and label which is the square and which is the rectangle.

How are they the same?

How are they different?

2. Make two different rectangles. Draw them here and label the length of each of the sides.

How are they the same?

How are they different?

Building Quadrilaterals (page 2 of 2)

Follow the directions below to make quadrilaterals with your straw building kit.

3. Make two different squares. Draw them here, and label the length of each of the sides.

How are they the same?

How are they different?

4. Make two different quadrilaterals that are not squares or rectangles. Draw them here, and label the length of each of the sides.

How are they the same?

How are they different?

Name Date

Finding Angles (page 1 of 2)

Use your straws to make angles of different sizes. Draw a picture of each angle you make. Then find 2 or 3 objects in the room that have angles that match these sizes, and record the name of each object.

1. Make a right angle (90 degrees).

Draw your angle.	Objects with this angle:

2. Make an angle that is smaller than a right angle.

Draw your angle.	Objects with this angle:

3. Make an angle that is larger than a right angle.

Draw your angle.	Objects with this angle:

Name Date

Finding Angles (page 2 of 2)

Use your straws to make angles of different sizes. Draw a picture of each angle you make. Then find 2 or 3 objects in the room that have angles that match these sizes, and record the name of each object.

4. Make an angle that is much smaller than a right angle.

Draw your angle.	Objects with this angle:

5. Make an angle that is much larger than a right angle.

Draw your angle.	Objects with this angle:

6. List at least three things you know about angles.
You may draw pictures if that will help you explain.

Name Date

Is It a Quadrilateral?

Look at each shape below. For each shape that is **not** a quadrilateral, explain why it is not one.

NOTE Students use their knowledge of properties of a quadrilateral to determine whether a shape is a quadrilateral and to explain why a shape is not a quadrilateral.

SMH 118, 121

Shape	This shape is not a quadrilateral because . . .
Example: 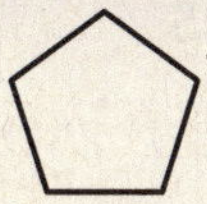	it has five sides.
1. 	
2. 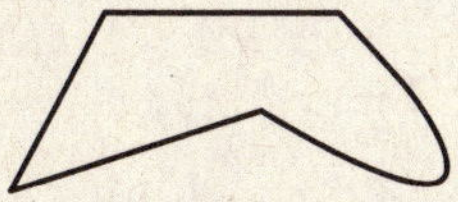	
3. 	
4. 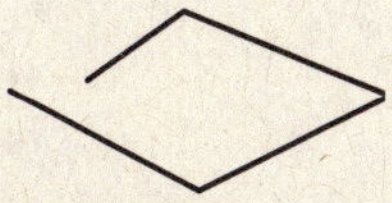	

Ongoing Review

5. Circle the statement that is **not** true.

A. A right angle has 90 degrees.
B. All quadrilaterals have 4 right angles.
C. A triangle can have a right angle.
D. All squares have right angles.

Building More Triangles and Quadrilaterals (page 1 of 2)

Follow the directions below to make triangles and quadrilaterals with your straw building kit. Draw a picture of each shape you make, and label the lengths of the straws you used for each side.

1. Make two different triangles that have all sides the same length.

2. Make a triangle that has a right angle.

3. Make a triangle that has three different side lengths.

Building More Triangles and Quadrilaterals (page 2 of 2)

4. Make a quadrilateral that has at least one right angle.

5. Make a quadrilateral that has at least one angle that is smaller than a right angle.

6. Make a quadrilateral that has at least one angle that is larger than a right angle.

Make $1.00, Make $2.00

NOTE Students practice finding combinations of amounts that add to a given total.

1. Fill in the blanks to make combinations of four amounts that add up to $1.00.

Example:

$0.25 + 0.25 + 0.40 + 0.10 = $1.00

______ + 0.15 + ______ + ______ = $1.00

______ + ______ + 0.10 + ______ = $1.00

______ + 0.30 + ______ + ______ = $1.00

2. Now fill in the blanks to make combinations of four amounts that add up to $2.00.

______ + 0.35 + ______ + ______ = $2.00

______ + ______ + 0.60 + ______ = $2.00

______ + ______ + ______ + 0.95 = $2.00

How Much Taller? How Much Longer?

NOTE Students compare heights and lengths in centimeters.

SMH **28, 32–35**

For each problem, write an equation, solve the problem, and show your solution. You may use number lines or drawings to help you explain your thinking.

1. Mr. Vega is 185 centimeters tall. Oscar is 129 centimeters tall. How much taller is Mr. Vega than Oscar?

2. An NBA basketball player is 216 centimeters tall. How much taller is the basketball player than Mr. Vega?

3. The Burmese python at the Midtown Zoo is 330 centimeters long. The boa constrictor is 217 centimeters long. How much longer is the Burmese python?

How Big Is Our Classroom?

NOTE Students identify and accurately measure the perimeter of a shape using U.S. Standard and metric units.

SMH 110–111, 112

1. Estimate how many yardstick lengths it will take to measure the perimeter of your classroom.
2. Multiply the number of yardsticks by 3 to get an accurate estimate of the perimeter in feet.
3. Measure the perimeter of the room as best you can. You may want to have one person measure with the yardstick and the other person keep a tally of how many yardstick lengths you use.
4. After you have measured the actual perimeter of your classroom, skip count or multiply by 3 to get the measurement in feet (instead of yards).

Answer the following questions:

1. How many yardstick lengths do you think it will take to find the perimeter of your classroom? ________
2. What do you estimate the perimeter of your classroom to be in feet? ________
3. How many yardstick lengths did it actually take to measure the perimeter of your classroom? ________
4. What is the perimeter of your classroom in feet? ________
5. Do you think you made an accurate estimate of the classroom's perimeter? Explain why or why not.

____

____